T0146570

Four Kinds of
SANCTIFICATION

Apostle William H. Bingham

WESTBOW
PRESS®
A DIVISION OF THOMAS NELSON
& ZONDERVAN

Scripture taken from the King James Version of the Bible.

WestBow Press books may be ordered through
booksellers or by contacting:

WestBow Press
A Division of Thomas Nelson & Zondervan
1663 Liberty Drive
Bloomington, IN 47403
www.westbowpress.com
1 (866) 928-1240

ISBN: 978-1-5127-4069-1 (sc)
ISBN: 978-1-5127-4070-7 (e)

Library of Congress Control Number: 2016907069

Print information available on the last page.

WestBow Press rev. date: 5/6/2016

Sanctification is to set perpetually in the consciousness and follow the Writs of the Gospel

Apostle William H. Bingham

2016

Saving faith is an immediate
relation to Christ, accepting,
receiving, resting upon
Him alone, for justification,
sanctification, and eternal life
by virtue of God's grace [1]
Charles Spurgeon

Contents

Acknowledgement

Acknowledgement goes to God foremost. To my Father and Mother Ruben and Mittie Bingham who is resting with Jesus, they taught me the principles of God. To my wife Ella Marie Bingham for 34 years of marriage, she constantly inspires and motivates me to stay the righteous course. Love you much honey. Special thanks go to Sister Debra Townsend and Martinise Bingham for assisting me with this project. Last but certainly not least, my Church family Perpetual Life, for your prayers and support. To all my children: DeJuan, Joseph, Christel, Rodney, Angela, Terry, Hershel and Harrold. To Apostle Skip and Alecia Horton thank you for your excellent teachings that, you imparted to our ministry. Finally, to my big brother Doctor Joe Cephus Bingham Sr., for your input and hours of labor, Love you Sir.

Foreword

The writers of the Old Testament uses SANCTIFY in various forms one-hundred and six times. However, the Gospel speaks of sanctification thirty-one separate occasions. The message denotes consecration in both Books. In layman's terms, consecrate is birth out of setting-apart or the condition to prearrange. Therefore, the definition shows classification in matters of position and relationship before God, and unrighteousness. Apostle Bingham is articulating a general interpretation of salvation. A more specific explanation is forthcoming.

Holiness, in diverse forms appears over four hundred times in the Old Testament and twelve in the Gospels. Less mention in the New Covenant has no significant, because devoutness and righteousness carries the same idea as SANCTIFY. God in the Body of Jesus Christ is Divine, harmless, undefiled, and separate from iniquity. As a result, His fundamental nature is righteous sanctification. Though, important to understand that each time

Holy and *Sanctify* appear in the Bible they do not suggest saint-ship.

For instance, the Patriarchs, Prophets, and their genealogies speak of Israel often as saints. In many occurrences, the Bible explains saintliness as mere human characteristics, but God relegates holiness to Christian's position on how they understand HIM. Therefore, sinners are never associated with righteousness and the quality of life enjoyed by Jehovah's people. The secular world uses the word sainted to complement the populace good conduct but flattering remarks dictates personage acceptance. When manners contradict their right morals, saint-ship reduces to hypocrisy.

So, righteous sainthood is not depending on human progression. Every born again person is a Glorified soul the moment he or she accepts Jesus. Study John Chapter 3. So, the entire Church of GOD, (IS) THE BODY OF CHRIST, He calls-out, and separate them hence they are the saints of this dispensation. When using the word sanctified in tandem with righteousness, expression of dedication to Jehovah is inevitable. However, because many followers do not know their position in THE LORD, they do not believe they are saints.

The name saint out trump all titles in the Bible except one:

- Brethren 184
- Saints 62
- Christians 3

The Means of Sanctification

God shows the foremost method of sanctification throughout the entire Bible. *Sanctify them through thy truth: thy word is truth.* [2] John 17:17. After acceptance of sainthood, The Author of The Scriptures gives an inheritance to every sanctified soul. See Acts 20: 32. Consecration is like seed. The plant life is in the kernel. Righteous living is in Jesus Christ. He who accepts the Gospel in their heart receives the Personality of The Beginning and The End. John 1: 11-12.

So sanctification is the vehicle means of sharing the Word. When saints witness righteousness, The Intercessor is present but the infinite holiness of the Father and Son are one with the individual. THEY classify, set apart, and separate transgressions from believers. The Almighty has the power to sanction sainthood because HE is Divine. Jesus Christ is the Holy Spirit and THEY BOTH are in JEHOVAH. Study John 10: 30, 17: 21. In HIM or (TRIAD THEM) Christians have their being and sanctification. Study Acts 17: 28.

Please study the Scriptures below to get a richer understanding.

The Triune God sanctifies

And such were some of you: but ye are washed, but ye are sanctified, but ye are justified in the name of the Lord Jesus, and by the Spirit of our God. [3]

1 Corinthians 6:11

The Father Sanctifies

And the very God of peace sanctify you wholly; and *I pray God* your whole spirit and soul and body be preserved blameless unto the coming of our Lord Jesus Christ. [4]

1 Thessalonians 5:23

The Son Sanctifies

That he might sanctify and cleanse it with the washing of water by the word. [5]

Ephesians 5:26

For both he that sanctifieth and they who sanctified *are* all of one: for which cause he is not ashamed to call them brethren [6]

Hebrews 2:11

Saying, I will declare thy name unto my brethren, in the midst of the church will I sing praise unto thee. [7]

Hebrews 2:12

Forasmuch then as the children are partakers of flesh and blood, he also himself likewise took part of the same; that through death he might destroy him that had the power of death, that is, the devil [8]

Hebrews 2:14 (KJV)

The Spirit sanctifies

[16] That I should be the minister of Jesus Christ to the Gentiles, ministering the gospel of God, that the offering up of the Gentiles might be acceptable, being sanctified by the Holy Ghost. [9]

Romans 15:16 (KJV)

[13] But we are bound to give thanks always to God for you, brethren beloved of the Lord, because God hath from the beginning chosen you to salvation through sanctification of the Spirit and belief of the truth [10]

2 Thessalonians 2:13 (KJV)

God the Father Sanctified the Son

36 Say ye of him, whom the Father hath sanctified, and sent into the world, Thou blasphemest; because I said, I am the Son of God? [11] John 10:36 (KJV)

God Sanctified the Priest and the People of Israel

Exodus 29:44

Sanctification Is the Will of Jehovah

3 For this is the will of God, *even* your sanctification, that ye should abstain from fornication [12]

1 Thessalonians 4:3

The Saints Sanctification from God Is Holy By Their Union with Christ

Unto the church of God which is at Corinth, to them that are sanctified in Christ Jesus, called *to be* saints, with all that in every place call upon the name of Jesus Christ our Lord, both theirs and ours. [13]

1 Corinthians 1:2

Sanctification Scriptures

- 1 Corinthians 1:30
- John 17:17
- 1 Timothy 4:5
- Hebrew 9:13
- Hebrews 13:12
- Hebrew 10:10
- 1 Peter 1:2
- Hebrew 12:14
- 2 Timothy 2: 21-22
- Acts 26:18

The Scriptures above are not exhaustible when proving sanctification. However, they show a clear picture of God's favor. So anybody can see consecration and holiness has its root meaning in righteousness. This includes places or building when set apart for THE LORD'S purposes. Old Testament sanctification had its connotation in setting aside the Tabernacle as a sanctified place of worship. Exodus 3: 5, Joshua 5: 15. The priest blessed the articles in the Tent for devotional purpose. When a person is Holy; his or her moral disposition is always transforming to righteousness. Where righteous qualities exist cleansing and purification is a prerequisite.

Introduction

Greek word for sanctification is Hagiazo, meaning to set-apart. As a result, Christians must be Holy for God's use. The believer's sanctification resonates by the truth of His Word. As they, study and practice righteousness THE LORD consecrate believers. As the Holy Writs, saturate supporters, their nature looks, and acts as Jesus Christ.

So they understand how he or she is to live and prosper by faith. 3 John 1: 2. As him and she lives for Christ, their sanctified souls will also present new and exciting challenges for them. In time of troubles, Jehovah shows them how to conform to the image of His Son. However, a person must repent their transgressions daily if sanctification will rule their innate spirit. Therefore, it is imperative to understand the four stages of sanctification.

Sanctification means God is at work in the Righteous lives. Under the Old Testament, the blood of animals was required to atone for sin. Sanctification is void unless it is under the covenant of shed blood. Jesus sheds His Precious Blood for mankind forgiveness and justification. Therefore, as believers move in covenant relationship with Him, they evolve to primary sanctification to positional sanctification and then prospective sanctification seals their understanding.

The Apostle Peter notes: sanctification is not happenstance hence Christians are the elect of God from the foundation of the world. 1 Peter 1: 1-2. Christ preserves each individual in the Body of Christ for righteous use. THE LORD settled the question of righteousness for mankind in the counsel of holiness. From Adam to Abraham, He maintained divine principles in the form of human seed. Therefore, men methods of approach to Him must be Holy. Everybody who yields themselves to Him, He reveals His purpose and plan for them. Jesus spoke of Himself as sanctified in John 17: 19. His followers are to be set apart from sin. Hence, people who believe in Him are reserved for GOD'S use.

Has it ever occurred to you that one hundred pianos all tuned to the same fork are automatically tuned to each other? They are of one accord by being tuned, not to each other, but to another standard to which each one must individually bow. So one hundred worshipers met together, each one looking away to Christ, are in heart nearer to each other than they could possibly be, were they to become 'unity' conscious and turn their eyes away from God to strive for closer fellowship. [14]

A.W. Tozer, The Pursuit of God

Chapter 1

Primary Sanctification

The Primary denotation of sanctification is: Set-aside inanimate or animate resources intended for a specific functioning by a creator. For instance, the shoemaker hallows his footgear to protect the feet. Protecting the extremities is the prime reason shoes. A carpenter builds and sanctifies homes to give a family shelter. Provided refuge from the elements is his cause for building. In the theological realm, anything used for Jehovah purpose is Holy. *And one cried unto another, and said, Holy, holy, holy, is the LORD of hosts: the whole earth is full of his glory.* [15] *Isaiah 6: 3.* Nothing shares Holiness with the Almighty. Study Leviticus 11: 44, Matthew 5: 44, and 1 Peter 1: 15-16.

So primary sanctification, connect believers to Jesus under THE FATHER'S protection. God took great care in sanctifying the Israelites' on the night of their

Passover. Note He gives them crucial instructions on how they should carry out their sanctified position without deviations.

And they shall take of the blood, and strike *it* on the two side posts and on the upper door post of the houses, wherein they shall eat it. [16]

Exodus 12:7

For I will pass through the land of Egypt this night, and will smite all the firstborn in the land of Egypt, both man and beast; and against all the gods of Egypt I will execute judgment: I *am* the LORD. [17]

Exodus 12:12

And the blood shall be to you for a token upon the houses where ye *are*: and when I see the blood, I will pass over you, and the plague shall not be upon you to destroy *you*, when I smite the land of Egypt. [18]

Exodus 12:13 (KJV)

The Israelite was to put sacrificial lamb's blood over their doorpost and on each side. The pureblood protected their house; therefore, whoever was in the house, Israelites, or Egyptians THE LORD'S consecration was upon them. Thus, righteousness hid them from the death angel. The dispensation of grace calls for sinners to repent and accept the conciliatory Blood of Jesus to purge their sins for all eternity. Every single Christian has the Vital Plasma of THE ANOINTED ONE over the pillars of their life after repentance.

Jehovah designated Apostle Bingham father and mother hence as a child under their roof, he was holy or sanctified. His parents dwelling habitation was a primary place of devotion, set-aside for worship. Though, he had not accepted Christ as Savior; he was in a sanctified home.

Apostle Bingham shared his life with sinner for a season but he never forgot his righteous home preparation. *Train up a child in the way he should go: and when he is old, he will not depart from it.* [19] Proverbs 22: 6. His consecrated parent's home was the tutor to put him on the path righteousness. Therefore, upon the call of Jesus Christ, his innate spirit would adhere and separate from the world. He thanks God, for the primary sanctified home training.

You have the fruit of the spirit in you, because when Christ comes in you everything he is and has comes with him as a seed as a seed as a seed as a seed. If we can ever understand this we can finally get over being confused about what the Bible says we have compared to our experience. Everything the Bible says we have we have it. As believers in Christ it is in us, but it comes as a SEED! The Bible actually calls Christ THE Seed. Capital "S". So, I like to put it like this: When Christ first comes into your life the seed of everything God is comes into your spirit. The Bible says that the image of Christ is captured in us and that we are destined, you have a destiny, a destiny to be molded into his image of Jesus Christ. Your destiny and my destiny is to get out into the world and act like Jesus. [20]

Joyce Meyer

Chapter 2

Positional Sanctification

Unto the church of God which is at Corinth, to them that are sanctified in Christ Jesus, called *to be* saints, with all that in every place call upon the name of Jesus Christ our Lord, both theirs and ours. [21]

1 Corinthians 1:2

Paul is writing to the problematic Churches at Corinth. There geographical location was in the Capital of the Southern Province of Achaia. The Romans destroyed this metropolis in 146 B.C., but because of its important ecological venue, they later rebuilt it under Julius Caesar in 46 B.C. By the time the Apostle arrived in the booming town 50 or 52 A.D., the seat of government had grown to a population of five hundred thousand people. On the highest point of the city stood the pagan temple of Aphrodite the goddess of love. Thousands went there to indulge themselves with prostitutes and idol worship.

Philosophy of Athens influenced the city, but it never rises as an intellectual culture. The citizen and tourists were too busy making and spending money to do academia theorizing. Many ethnicities settled there since it was the mercantile center of that region. So as immigrants unpacked their bags, they too uncrates their pagan gods,

Corinth became a cosmopolitan city with attending heathen vices attached to the population. Even though, the city was environmental sociable for travelers, trade, and Polytheism worship it was for naught. Hence, today just the ruins of the city stands and their idols vanished altogether. Though, the Word that the Apostle Paul preached is yet standing strong. *Heaven and earth shall pass away, but my words shall not pass away.* [22] *Matthew 24: 35.*

In spite their freethinking skepticism about The Unknown God; THE LORD positioned His Church there. *For as I passed by, and beheld your devotions, I found an altar with this inscription, TO THE UNKNOWN GOD. Whom therefore ye ignorantly worship, him declare I unto you.* [23] *Study* Acts 17: 23. The Beloved Son position His followers in Him to witness to sinners, not alienate them. The Apostle Paul was a devout Christian, but not always the case. Before salvation, he persecuted the house of Worship and put many Christians to death. When THE ALMIGHTY met this Benjamite (Philippians 3: 5) on the road to Damascus (Acts 9: 3-6) he took up a stance to protect the Law from supporters of Christ.

The Matchless Light of The Redeemer was so bright the Apostle falls to the ground. Then the Anointed One asked him a searching inquiry that recounts with every sinner who comes to HIM. WHY PERSECUTE ME? Note Paul made an inquest he beforehand knew the answer to: <u>WHO ART THOU LORD</u>? The Author of the Scriptures explains: Jesus hence this self-righteous Pharisees trembled with blameless fear and said: LORD what do YOU want me to do? The King of Kings charged him to go into the city to get his positional orders from the Prophet Ananias.

After Paul's Conversion, he disappeared in the desert (Galatians 1: 11-24) for three years where the Counselor instructed him on the life, death, and resurrection of Jesus Christ. *The Comforter which is the Holy Ghost, whom the Father will send in my name, he shall teach you all things, and bring all things to your remembrance, whatsoever I have said unto you.* [24] John 14: 26. He emerges from the wilderness as an Apostle of grace. He trades his post occupation as the keeper of the Law and writes two thirds of the

New Testament. Paul was human as every humanoid are but the question is: have every believer situated themselves in their righteous purpose?

A believer must position himself in Christ before taking on ministry witnessing. True, The Author of The Scriptures calls evildoers out of darkness into the marvelous light and situate them in Him. However, to understand their goal in full, saints have to spend time with the Almighty. For instance, Apostle Bingham worked at different vocations: schoolteacher, Greyhound Bus driver, pastry chef, and staff business manager. It took abundant patient to master each of the above skills. Nonetheless, those callings were not his life's mission. God called him as an Apostle, a Wilderness voice crying out the riches of the Prince of Peace to HIS chosen-sinners. Much prayer and fasting is still necessary to be worthy and positioned to carry the touch of Apostleship.

A superficial study of Ephesians 4: 11-12 could mislead the readers to think Apostles, Prophets, Evangelists, Shepherds, and Teachers functions outside the Sanctuary of Christ. Nevertheless, THE LORD gives them to His Church for developing the Body as a universal whole (v. 12). Verse 16 shows they too build the house of worship up from inside out. They too are part of House of Worship, as ministering members, so the entire congregation receives edification holistically.

As The Author of Eternal Salvation sanctified Paul to evangelize, He has positioned every righteous soul to do the same. The method of positional sanctification is the Doctrine of Good News to the Gentiles and everyone in the utmost parts of earth. In Luke Chapter 4: 18 Jesus noted: *The spirit of THE LORD was upon Him, because he anointed Him to preach the Gospel to the poor.* The Greek word for anoint is *Chrio* meaning to consecrate or sanctify. Therefore, The Redeemer is calling His people out of darkness and positioning them to share His Teachings. Hebrews 13: 16. Profession is that innate permanent place in God where Satan day and night tries to remove Christians from righteousness.

Paul's Epistles to the problematic Churches at Corinth shows the righteous cannot wallow in mire and expect liberation from misconduct. So, the Apostle purpose is for the universal Church of Jesus Christ is obvious: sanctification do not dwell with backsliders. 1 Corinthians Chapters 1 – 6. He rebukes a small faction who was relegating sin and grace is tolerable. THE LORD positioned His people for righteousness not transgressions. His Letters brings unity out of division. 1 Corinthians 1: 10 thru 4: 21.

Now I beseech you, brethren, by the name of our Lord Jesus Christ, that ye all speak the same thing, and *that* there be no divisions among you; but *that* ye be perfectly joined together in the same mind and in the same judgment. [25]

1 Corinthians 1:10

Although the Church at Corinth had problems, the Apostle Paul addresses them as sanctified souls. Their position in Jehovah had not changed even though their behavior needed correction. So, positional purification is holiness extrapolating sainthood through the Body and Shed Blood of Alpha and Omega.

Therefore, sanctification and consecration is distinctive classification through the saving grace of Jesus Christ that relegates facts about supporters' belief in THE LORD. As a result, every believer is sanctified and righteous before The King of kings. Irreproachable or humane living bears no relationship with holiness but moral principles should inspire him or she to live consecrated. The Christian position is the greatest incentive to be Holy.

The Epistles' Doctrine observes moralistic order. All Twenty One Letters exemplifies the majestic saving power of Jehovah. Then, concludes with an appeal to a life that corresponds with unity in Christ: (Romans 12: 1, Ephesians 4: 1, and Corinthians 3: 1). So:

- He accepts and positions every saint in Him.
- He is the believers' Position for righteousness.
- He redeems sinners and Christians from sin and positions them for eternity.
- He positions and sanctifies His supporters to do good works.
- He made Himself sanctification for His followers.

Therefore, positional sanctification makes followers as perfect as THE Author of the Scriptures without fault. Their posture in THE LORD sets them apart with Him.

A righteous place in The Almighty God justifies the weakest and strongest saints alike. Acts 20: 32, 1 Corinthians 6: 11, Hebrew 10: 10-14, and Jude Chapter One. Jehovah never gives His followers a license to sin. Though, the disparity of their sin nature does not neutralize their moral standing with Him. Study 1 Corinthians Chapters 5 - 6: 8. The Blood of Jesus Christ covers every soul that believes in Him. Hebrew 10: 10, Ephesians 4: 24. IF, anybody is serving a god that cannot keep them try JESUS. John 3: 16.

The Pentecostal power, when you sum it all up, is just more of God's love. If it does not bring more love, it is simply a counterfeit. [26]

William J. Seymour

Chapter 3

Practical Sanctification

Sanctify them through thy truth: thy WORD is truth [27]

John 17:17

Sanctification is that empirical paradigm that predicates blameless preservation. Then, God uses the pure in heart to reach sinners but everything set aside for His cause pleases Him. For instance, the Seven Furnishings of the Tabernacle were reserve for righteous purpose. Study Exodus Chapters 25 thru 40. Even the ground can be Holy: Exodus 3: 5. Jesus unwavering in righteousness satisfies His Father. He was faithful to holiness because He shed His Precious Blood for mankind forgiveness and justification. Romans 5: 1, Matthew 6: 14-15.

Sanctification is undertaking and unmitigated but an ongoing progression in chorus. As a result, every believer is Holy through the sacrificial work of Jesus Christ. Though, the sinner plays no active part in redemption until he or she hears, believes, and trusts The Author of The Scriptures. Then their deliverance is a onetime inductive act whereby they become vessels of honor, practical for Kingdom minded and Kingdom living.

If a man therefore purge himself from these, he shall be a vessel unto honour, sanctified, and meet for the master's use, and prepared unto every good work. [28]

2 Timothy 2:21

So, practical sanctification is essential for believers' daily life, since righteous practicalities are inherent inviolability that comes by Holy Writs. For example, THE LORD said, *sanctify them in the truth, thy word is truth.* John 17: 17. The Scriptures provides all the help and guidance that saints need. *Wherewithal shall a young man cleanse his way?* Psalm 119: 9-16. His question is rhetorical: By attentiveness to the Gospel of Jesus Christ. THE LORD'S infallibility cleanses and make free simultaneously. Believers solidified in Godliness hence sin is no problem.

The Almighty has purposed parishioners to be instruments of compassion. He says unequivocal: *You are not your own.* Study 1 Corinthians 6: 20. Practical sanctification is a daily washing in righteousness. So saints must practice speaking the Word in their lives and others. In January 2010, a physician diagnosed Apostle Bingham with prostate cancer. After he received the news, he was in denial but after several opinions and the same result; he gave the okay for radiation therapy. His holistic homilies' were on the restorative power of Jesus Christ and he saw many healings. However, he allowed the *spirit of fear* (2 Timothy 1: 7) to come upon him when the doctors describe the side effects of radioactive particles.

Even so, he spoke the Word of God over his body according to Apostle Paul's Letter to young Pastor Timothy. He encourages him to live by faith and not out of trepidation. *Let us hold fast the profession of our faith without wavering; for he is faithful that promised.* [29] Hebrews 10:23. After Apostle Bingham talked with THE LORD, the enemy come and snatches it from him. So the Holy Spirit inspired him after speaking practice holding firm the promises hence they in tandem capitulates a sound mind. As he continued to practice and speak, he would ignore adverse circumstances and notice how ministering angels move at the command.

Then said the LORD unto me, Thou hast well seen: for I will hasten my word to perform it. [30]

Jeremiah 1: 12

Confidence in precept upon precepts of God keeps believers from sinning against Him.

Thy word have I hid in mine heart, that I might not sin against thee. [31]

Psalm 119: 11

Sacred Writ in hart is practical sanctification implementing righteous compassion. Study Romans 1: 16 thru Chapters 5. Paul's Letter to the Romans shows how a sinner receives sainthood from Christ and stand vindicated before Jehovah. As a result, he, or she has eternal deliverance from the penalty of transgressions forever. The doctrine of Justification introduces cognitive thoughts to the mind so humans can know the value of salvation. The meaning *justified* in all practicality is distinct or preserved for blamelessness.

For followers of Jesus Christ, blameworthiness means The King of kings, forgive their sins, and impute to them the Holiness of His Son. Note their purification comes through practical faith in The Author of Eternal Salvation alone. Romans 5: 1, Galatians 3: 24. Nobody can earn His deliverance from sin through works. Ephesians 2: 8, Titus 3: 5. The righteousness that The Alpha and Omega give stands on faithful Principles from Genesis to Revelation. Therefore, when sinners accept Him as

Lord, they are justified by faith; however, they must exercise righteous conviction every day.

Practical Sanctification is the day-by-day application for believers. This includes fellowshipping, reconciling, and formulating relationships with other Christians.

And they continued stedfastly in the apostles' doctrine and fellowship, and in breaking of bread, and in prayers. [32]

Acts 2: 42

And be ye kind one to another, tenderhearted, forgiving one another, even as God for Christ's sake hath forgiven you. [33]

Ephesians 4: 32

I beseech you therefore, brethren, by the mercies of God, that ye present your bodies a living sacrifice, holy, acceptable unto God, *which is* your reasonable service. And be not conformed to this world: but be ye transformed by the renewing of your mind, that ye may prove what *is* that good, and acceptable, and perfect, will of God. [34]

Romans 12: 1-2

Jehovah's attitude for the unsaved is unambiguous. The righteous are to exemplify straightforward morality towards government leaders and all people. Romans 13: 1. Separation to THE CREATOR is disunion from defilement. As a result, Christian's practical sanctification begins at the time of conversion.

Unto the church of God which is at Corinth, to them that are sanctified in Christ Jesus, called *to be* saints, with all that in every place call upon the name of Jesus Christ our Lord, both theirs and ours. [35]

1 Corinthians 1:2

So, practical consecration results from yielding to The Prince of Peace, ones total dedication. Romans 12: 1. Again, by doing so, supporters classify themselves as set-aside for kingdom building. Righteous perseverance leaves no room for unrighteousness. Romans 6: 22. The Bible takes into account the sins of every Christian but grace gives no one a license to do wrong. However, it makes forgiving contingency for saints who make mistakes. Atonement is freedom from transgressions. *Thy word have I hid in mine heart, that I might not sin against thee.* [36] Psalm 119: 11.

Humanity will continue unrighteousness as long as they abide in these bodies. The sinful disposition did not receive salvation simultaneously with the innate spirit. Romans 7: 21, 1 John 1: 8. Scripture never promises eradication of the sin nature, but as believers submit to their righteous temperament, he or she can enjoy many moments of victories. Galatians 5: 16-23. All supporters have died unto immoral acts because of Christ's death. So, followers must die to iniquity. Cognitive reframing from immorality is every believer responsibility, Romans 6: 1-14.

Practical sanctification aids in wisdom, knowledge, understanding, and grace. Absolve consecration relegates to the highest holiness. Therefore, Christians may live irreproachable, but not without fault. For example, a child who struggles to form his first cursive letters is blameless yet his or her writing is not faultless. They still must practice to prefect a legible style. Saints will make mistakes in these imperfect bodies. *For now we see through a glass, darkly; but then face to face: now I know in part; but then shall I know even as also I am known.* [37] 1 Corinthians 13: 12.

All believers are living in the light and experience that can be their tomorrow. For this reason, righteousness must be their practical application every day. *...they that are Christ's have crucified the flesh with the affections and lusts.* [38] So there is perfection within imperfection.

Chapter 4

Prospective Sanctification

And the very God of peace sanctify you wholly; and *I pray God* your whole spirit and soul and body be preserved blameless unto the coming of our Lord Jesus Christ. [39]

1 Thessalonians 5:23

The Apostle Paul basis for addressing the Church at Thessalonica; Gnosticism had infiltrated their Worship Centers. The Greek term is gnosis is KNOWLEDGE. They depreciate the value of the material world and exalted the soul or mind. They believe the soul separates at death since the body is temporal. However, their most fallacious doctrine is spiritual knowledge is available to those with superior intellect. Therefore, they treat faith with contempt and salvation comes by knowledge alone.

Paul wanted them to understand the body is the Prospective temple of Holy Spirit. 1 Corinthians 6: 19.

Prospective Sanctification Is Christianity Glorification

God's definitive resolve is reminding believers they are: *...the sons of God and it doth not yet appear what we shall be: but we know that, when he shall appear, we shall be like him; for we shall see him as he is.* [40] 1 John 3: 2. The Apostle Paul's Letter to the Romans points out supporters of Christ must...BE conformed to the likeness of Jehovah's Son. Romans 8: 29. As a result, The Author of Eternal Salvation will have the first place in their lives.

Paul understood prospective sanctification as the logistical pinnacle for God's eternal plan of redemption. Romans 4: 17. The Apostle also noticed, *The fundamental fact of existence is that this trust in God, this faith, is the firm foundation under everything that makes life worth living. It's our handle on what we can't see.* [41] *Hebrews 11:1.* So, man's perspective sanctification is already in the past for mankind since former and future is part of THE LORD'S unchanging decree. That is, He is Omniscience and sees the past and future simultaneously. Perspective sanctification is why Paul writes. And we know that all things work together for good to them that love God, to them who are the called according to *his* purpose. [42] Romans 8:28. He understood himself and all believers as constant objects of God's will.

Therefore, prospective sanctification recounts Christian's final perfection that implodes in Glory with The Absolute Being. By His grace and transforming power, He changes the righteous holistically to be like Him. He will present them faultless:

And the very God of peace sanctify you wholly; and *I pray God* your whole spirit and soul and body be preserved blamcless unto the coming of our Lord Jesus Christ. [43]

1 Thessalonians 5:23 (KJV)

Now unto him that is able to keep you from falling, and to present *you* faultless before the presence of his glory with exceeding joy, [25] To the only wise God our Saviour, *be* glory and majesty, dominion and power, both now and ever. Amen. [44]

Jude 24-25

Jude assures followers of Jesus that He...is able to do exceeding abundantly above all that we ask or think... [45] Ephesians 3: 20. He is going to keep His people not because of their righteousness but because of Christ Who lives in them. Proverbs 24: 16 say, for a just *man* falleth seven times, and riseth up again: but the wicked shall fall into mischief. [46] Proverbs 24:16 He is going to present the righteous before His Father faultless.

While I was with them in the world, I kept them in thy name: those that thou gavest me I have kept, and none of them is lost, but the son of perdition; that the scripture might be fulfilled. [47]

John 17:12 (KJV)

Humiliation is the beginning of sanctification; and as without this, without holiness, no man will see God, though he pore whole nights upon his Bible; so without humility, no man shall hear God speak to his soul, though he hear three two-hour sermons each day [48]

John Donne

Endnotes

1   http://www.christianquotes.info/quotes-by-topic/
    quotes-about-sanctification/
2   *The Holy Bible : King James Version.* electronic ed. of the
    1769 edition of the 1611 Authorized Version. Bellingham
    WA : Logos Research Systems, Inc., 1995
3   *The Holy Bible : King James Version.* electronic ed. of the
    1769 edition of the 1611 Authorized Version. Bellingham
    WA : Logos Research Systems, Inc., 1995
4   *The Holy Bible : King James Version.* electronic ed. of the
    1769 edition of the 1611 Authorized Version. Bellingham
    WA : Logos Research Systems, Inc., 1995
5   *The Holy Bible : King James Version.* electronic ed. of the
    1769 edition of the 1611 Authorized Version. Bellingham
    WA : Logos Research Systems, Inc., 1995
6   *The Holy Bible : King James Version.* electronic ed. of the
    1769 edition of the 1611 Authorized Version. Bellingham
    WA : Logos Research Systems, Inc., 1995
7   *The Holy Bible : King James Version.* electronic ed. of the
    1769 edition of the 1611 Authorized Version. Bellingham
    WA : Logos Research Systems, Inc., 1995
8   *The Holy Bible : King James Version.* electronic ed. of the
    1769 edition of the 1611 Authorized Version. Bellingham
    WA : Logos Research Systems, Inc., 1995

[9]   *The Holy Bible : King James Version.* electronic ed. of the 1769 edition of the 1611 Authorized Version. Bellingham WA : Logos Research Systems, Inc., 1995

[10] *The Holy Bible : King James Version.* electronic ed. of the 1769 edition of the 1611 Authorized Version. Bellingham WA : Logos Research Systems, Inc., 1995

[11] *The Holy Bible : King James Version.* electronic ed. of the 1769 edition of the 1611 Authorized Version. Bellingham WA : Logos Research Systems, Inc., 1995

[12] *The Holy Bible : King James Version.* electronic ed. of the 1769 edition of the 1611 Authorized Version. Bellingham WA : Logos Research Systems, Inc., 1995

[13] *The Holy Bible : King James Version.* electronic ed. of the 1769 edition of the 1611 Authorized Version. Bellingham WA : Logos Research Systems, Inc., 1995

[14] http://www.goodreads.com/quotes/tag/sanctification

[15] *The Holy Bible : King James Version.* electronic ed. of the 1769 edition of the 1611 Authorized Version. Bellingham WA : Logos Research Systems, Inc., 1995

[16] *The Holy Bible : King James Version.* electronic ed. of the 1769 edition of the 1611 Authorized Version. Bellingham WA : Logos Research Systems, Inc., 1995

[17] *The Holy Bible : King James Version.* electronic ed. of the 1769 edition of the 1611 Authorized Version. Bellingham WA : Logos Research Systems, Inc., 1995

[18] *The Holy Bible : King James Version.* electronic ed. of the 1769 edition of the 1611 Authorized Version. Bellingham WA : Logos Research Systems, Inc., 1995

[19] *The Holy Bible : King James Version.* electronic ed. of the 1769 edition of the 1611 Authorized Version. Bellingham WA : Logos Research Systems, Inc., 1995

[20] http://www.goodreads.com/quotes/tag/sanctification

[21] *The Holy Bible : King James Version.* electronic ed. of the 1769 edition of the 1611 Authorized Version. Bellingham WA : Logos Research Systems, Inc., 1995

22 *The Holy Bible : King James Version.* electronic ed. of the
    1769 edition of the 1611 Authorized Version. Bellingham
    WA : Logos Research Systems, Inc., 1995

23 *The Holy Bible : King James Version.* electronic ed. of the
    1769 edition of the 1611 Authorized Version. Bellingham
    WA : Logos Research Systems, Inc., 1995

24 *The Holy Bible : King James Version.* electronic ed. of the
    1769 edition of the 1611 Authorized Version. Bellingham
    WA : Logos Research Systems, Inc., 1995

25 *The Holy Bible : King James Version.* electronic ed. of the
    1769 edition of the 1611 Authorized Version. Bellingham
    WA : Logos Research Systems, Inc., 1995

26 ...https://www.google.com/search?q=quotes+on+
    sanctification&biw=1024&bih=544&tbm=isch&tbo=
    u&source=univ&sa=X&sqi=2&ved=0ahUKEwjHmrKXk
    O3JAhUJ6yYKHYgNDWUQsAQIMQ

27 *The Holy Bible : King James Version.* electronic ed. of the
    1769 edition of the 1611 Authorized Version. Bellingham
    WA : Logos Research Systems, Inc., 1995

28 *The Holy Bible : King James Version.* electronic ed. of the
    1769 edition of the 1611 Authorized Version. Bellingham
    WA : Logos Research Systems, Inc., 1995

29 *The Holy Bible : King James Version.* electronic ed. of the
    1769 edition of the 1611 Authorized Version. Bellingham
    WA : Logos Research Systems, Inc., 1995

30 *The Holy Bible : King James Version.* electronic ed. of the
    1769 edition of the 1611 Authorized Version. Bellingham
    WA : Logos Research Systems, Inc., 1995

31 *The Holy Bible : King James Version.* electronic ed. of the
    1769 edition of the 1611 Authorized Version. Bellingham
    WA : Logos Research Systems, Inc., 1995

32 *The Holy Bible : King James Version.* electronic ed. of the
    1769 edition of the 1611 Authorized Version. Bellingham
    WA : Logos Research Systems, Inc., 1995

[33]   *The Holy Bible : King James Version.* electronic ed. of the 1769 edition of the 1611 Authorized Version. Bellingham WA : Logos Research Systems, Inc., 1995

[34]   *The Holy Bible : King James Version.* electronic ed. of the 1769 edition of the 1611 Authorized Version. Bellingham WA : Logos Research Systems, Inc., 1995

[35]   *The Holy Bible : King James Version.* electronic ed. of the 1769 edition of the 1611 Authorized Version. Bellingham WA : Logos Research Systems, Inc., 1995

[36]   *The Holy Bible : King James Version.* electronic ed. of the 1769 edition of the 1611 Authorized Version. Bellingham WA : Logos Research Systems, Inc., 1995

[37]   *The Holy Bible : King James Version.* electronic ed. of the 1769 edition of the 1611 Authorized Version. Bellingham WA : Logos Research Systems, Inc., 1995

[38]   *The Holy Bible : King James Version.* electronic ed. of the 1769 edition of the 1611 Authorized Version. Bellingham WA : Logos Research Systems, Inc., 1995

[39]   *The Holy Bible : King James Version.* electronic ed. of the 1769 edition of the 1611 Authorized Version. Bellingham WA : Logos Research Systems, Inc., 1995

[40]   *The Holy Bible : King James Version.* electronic ed. of the 1769 edition of the 1611 Authorized Version. Bellingham WA : Logos Research Systems, Inc., 1995

[41]   Peterson, Eugene H.: *The Message : The Bible in Contemporary Language.* Colorado Springs, Colo. : NavPress, 2002

[42]   *The Holy Bible : King James Version.* electronic ed. of the 1769 edition of the 1611 Authorized Version. Bellingham WA : Logos Research Systems, Inc., 1995

[43]   *The Holy Bible : King James Version.* electronic ed. of the 1769 edition of the 1611 Authorized Version. Bellingham WA : Logos Research Systems, Inc., 1995

[44]   *The Holy Bible : King James Version.* electronic ed. of the 1769 edition of the 1611 Authorized Version. Bellingham WA : Logos Research Systems, Inc., 1995

45 *The Holy Bible : King James Version.* electronic ed. of the
    1769 edition of the 1611 Authorized Version. Bellingham
    WA : Logos Research Systems, Inc., 1995
46 *The Holy Bible : King James Version.* electronic ed. of the
    1769 edition of the 1611 Authorized Version. Bellingham
    WA : Logos Research Systems, Inc., 1995
47 *The Holy Bible : King James Version.* electronic ed. of the
    1769 edition of the 1611 Authorized Version. Bellingham
    WA : Logos Research Systems, Inc., 1995
48 ...https://www.google.com/search?q=quotes+on+
    sanctification&biw=1024&bih=544&tbm=isch&tbo=
    u&source=univ&sa=X&sqi=2&ved=0ahUKEwjHmrKXk
    O3JAhUJ6yYKHYgNDWUQsAQIMQ#imgrc=_

About the Author

Apostle William H. Bingham born in 1950 but received his second transformation of soul change in 1977. He and Pastor Ella Bingham celebrated thirty-two-years of marriage in 2015. They are honored parents of eight children and a host of grandchildren.

He has traveled throughout the country ministering The Holy Scriptures to many denominations. THE LORD empowered him with the vision: Kingdom Minded for Kingdom Living to elevate His people to a higher calling. Then educate them on how they must energetically witness for the Kingdom of God. He knew there was a need for more Biblical training in his life, so he enrolled at Grace University in Omaha, Nebraska in 1981. Apostle Bingham studied with Grace, three and a half years until accepting Senior Pastor Position, at Perpetual Life Christian Ministries St. Louis, Missouri.

Therefore, he enrolled the Glad Tidings Bible College, where he finished his Undergraduate, and Graduate studies in 1992. In 2002, they ordained as Bishop, by Archbishop Joe Cephus Bingham under the Diocese of Perpetual Tidings. In 2012, his calling reached another pinnacle: Apostle H L Skip Horton ordained him to the office of Apostle.

Printed in the United States
By Bookmasters